Let's Look at ADVERTS

Elaine Canham

OXFORD
UNIVERSITY PRESS

OXFORD
UNIVERSITY PRESS

Great Clarendon Street, Oxford OX2 6DP

Oxford University Press is a department of the University of Oxford.
It furthers the University's objective of excellence in research, scholarship,
and education by publishing worldwide in

Oxford   New York

Auckland   Cape Town   Dar es Salaam   Hong Kong   Karachi
Kuala Lumpur   Madrid   Melbourne   Mexico City   Nairobi
New Delhi   Shanghai   Taipei   Toronto

With offices in

Argentina   Austria   Brazil   Chile   Czech Republic   France   Greece
Guatemala   Hungary   Italy   Japan   Poland   Portugal   Singapore
South Korea   Switzerland   Thailand   Turkey   Ukraine   Vietnam

Oxford is a registered trade mark of Oxford University Press
in the UK and in certain other countries

British Library Cataloguing in Publication Data

Data available

ISBN 978-0-19-919866-5

15 17 19 20 18 16 14

Printed in China by Imago

Paper used in the production of this book is a natural,
recyclable product made from wood grown in sustainable forests.
The manufacturing process conforms to the environmental
regulations of the country of origin

Acknowledgements

The publisher would like to thank the following for permission to reproduce
photographs: p6 Ancient Art & Architecture (top), Mary Evans Picture Library; p7
Ancient Art & Architecture, Bodleian Library; pp8 & 9 Advertising Archive; p10
Mary Evans Picture Library; pp11, 12, 13, 14, 15 Advertising Archive; p16 Picture
Post/Hulton Archive/Getty Images; pp17, 18, 19 Advertising Archive

Cover photo: Retna/Brandon O'Sullivan

Illustrations by Stefan Chabluk and Mark Draisey

Design by Andy Wilson

Contents

Introduction

Look carefully at the pages of this book – if you are really lucky you will find a £5 note. If you don't find one, come back to this page.

Advertising is all about
persuading
you to buy something you hadn't thought of trying before. If you hadn't thought you might find some money, would you have looked at all the pages in this book?

Adults get these kinds of offers all the time. For example, car companies sometimes send out letters with a key in them – all you have to do is go along to the showroom and see if your key fits. If it does, you can claim the car. If not, you can try driving it anyway. The company hopes, of course, that after seeing and driving the car you might want to buy it.

(Okay, so you didn't find a £5 note, but you have found something – **how advertising works.**)

4

Does your key fit?

Drive your new _Panther Cruiser_ away today!

Here's all you need to do:

1 **Bring this key to your nearest Deluxe car showroom**

2 **Place it in the ignition of our new model _Panther Cruiser_**

3 **If it starts, the car is yours!**

Don't delay – you could be driving your new car home today!

These kinds of adverts are called promotions. By giving something away, they make you think about a **product**.

History of advertising

There has always been advertising. As soon as there were shops, shopkeepers put signs above their doors so that people could tell from a distance what they sold. Even now, you can sometimes see a striped pole outside a barber's shop.

Pictures of adverts for property to rent more than two thousand years ago have been found painted on a wall in Rome. There is another picture, advertising an inn, painted on a wall in Pompeii, the ancient Roman city where volcanic ash from an eruption has preserved scenes of everyday life.

Barbers have red and white striped poles, because in the Middle Ages they used to carry out operations too, and hung bloody cloths on a stick outside their shops. The red and white is a **symbol** of that time.

There have been street criers shouting about what's going on in the town for hundreds, if not thousands of years.

In 1477 William Caxton printed what could be described as Britain's first advert, for a religious book called 'The Pyes of Salisbury'. He stuck posters on church doors claiming the book was cheap to buy.

If it plese ony man spirituel or temporel to bye ony pyes of two and thre comemoracios of salisburi vse enpryntid after the forme of this preset lettre whiche ben wel and truly correct, late hym come to westmo; nester in to the almonesrye at the reed pale and he shal haue them good chepe ∴

Suplico stet cedula

However, advertising was not the same as we know it today. Most people were too poor to afford to buy lots of things, and not many people could read.

Selling to the Victorians

In the early 1800s more and more machines and factories were built and lots of people began to work in them and earn money. This was called the **industrial revolution**. Britain became the richest country on Earth when it built up its **empire** under Queen Victoria. More people had more money to spend and more things to spend it on.

Then after it became the law in 1870 for children to go to school, more people were able to read. The sales of newspapers rocketed and advertising really took off.

Victorians called their adverts 'puffs and pushes'. A 'puff' told you about a product, while a 'push' tried to make you buy it. Can you work out what the 'puffs and pushes' are in the adverts on these pages?

8

The International Fur Store.

GENTLEMEN'S FUR-LINED OVERCOATS

ready for immediate wear.

New Designs in Three-Quarter and Full-Length

DRIVING OR TRAVELLING COATS
for Ladies,

IN SEAL OR CLOTH,

LINED SABLE, MINK OR MUSQUASH.

Only Address—

163 & 165, REGENT STREET, LONDON, W.

Victorians advertised in lots of different ways.
They painted signs on factories, made up songs,
produced posters, and used street criers, newspapers
and magazines to advertise their products.

Famous faces

Famous Victorians were used to help advertise things – just like famous people are today. This is called endorsement.

Famous actresses and singers were used, but the ultimate celebrity endorsement of the day was the Queen herself.

Queen Victoria features in an advert for printing inks in her Diamond Jubilee year.

Victorian newspaper adverts, like the one for a carpet sweeper on page 8, look dull because they were always printed in black and white. But in the 1870s the Victorians discovered how to produce cheap colour posters, which became popular for advertising.

Nowadays, sporting heroes like England's football champion, David Beckham, are paid millions of pounds to endorse things like mobile phones and sunglasses. Companies are happy to pay him because their sales go up. Just seeing a famous person using the product can make people want it. Of course, it doesn't necessarily mean that these things are the best there are.

POLICE
sunglasses
at
David Clulow
opticians

11

The appeal of adverts

The style of adverts has kept changing since Victorian times. In the last 100 years people have had more money to spend and our way of life has changed dramatically. People today buy cars and fridges and microwave ovens – all sorts of things that the Victorians didn't have.

However, whatever time you live in, adverts are always about persuading you to buy something.

In Victorian times, the differences between the wealthy and poor were very obvious. There was a lot of **snobbery**. Advertisers who wanted to appeal to women tried to show that their product would be something a lady would buy.

In the 1950s and 1960s Russia and America were beginning to send astronauts into space. Advertisers tried to sell things by showing people living **high-tech** futuristic lives. Nowadays adverts appeal to people's desire to look rich, stylish, cool, young and attractive.

Comparing old and new

Let's look at a modern advert for a lip gloss and a Victorian one for skin cream.

This is a Victorian advert for a skin cream.

SOFT WHITE HANDS.

BEETHAM'S Glycerine & Cucumber

Preserves the Skin from the effects of the SUN, Cold Winds, Hard Water, and Inferior Soaps.

Entirely Removes and Prevents all Redness Roughness, Tan, Irritation, &c., &c., and keeps the Skin Soft and Blooming in all weathers.

The *Queen* says :— "BEETHAM'S GLYCERINE and CUCUMBER is at all times safe. It keeps the hands delicately white and soft."

The *Lady's Pictorial* says :— "BEETHAM'S GLYCERINE and CUCUMBER is unrivalled in its marvellous effects upon the complexion."

The *Lady* says :— "BEETHAM'S GLYCERINE and CUCUMBER will be found most comforting and healing to the skin."

"Always young, always fair."

A BEAUTIFUL COMPLEXION

ensured by the use of BEETHAM'S Glycerine and Cucumber which is perfectly harmless, and may be applied to the skin of the tenderest infant. LADIES will find it Invaluable at all Seasons of the Year for Keeping the

SKIN SOFT, SMOOTH, AND WHITE.

REFUSE ALL IMITATIONS, MANY OF WHICH ARE POISONOUS. Be sure to Ask for 'BEETHAM'S,' THE ONLY GENUINE.

SOLD by ALL CHEMISTS and PERFUMERS in Bottles, 1s. and 2s. 6d. Either size sent Post Free for 3d. extra, by the Sole Makers, M. BEETHAM and SON, Chemists, CHELTENHAM.

Isn't it complicated? It has lots of fancy words and phrases, and sounds rather pompous. But it was appealing to women who wanted to be lady-like. It uses lady-like words like 'soft' and 'blooming'. It tells women the cream will make their hands soft and white because a real lady never went out in the sun or worked.

Advertisers also like to persuade us that we need something we have never heard of before. If they didn't tell us about lip gloss, or cheese and pickle flavour crisps, or fruity smelling pens, would we ask for them in the shops? Do we really *need* them?

This is a modern advert for lip gloss.

LIP REPAIR, NOT LIP SERVICE

The quick, effective solution to the problem of sore, chapped lips is here, NIVEA Lip Care Repair. This advanced formula contains Bisabolol, Panthenol and Vitamin E, which soothes, moisturises and regenerates your lips and helps prevent these problems recurring. Use it regularly and you won't be paying for lip service, just powerful, effective lip care that works for you every time.

NIVEA *Careline* **0800 616977** (1 800 409576 REPUBLIC OF IRELAND)

NIVEA
Lip Care

REPAIR

Care for sore
chapped lips

Much simpler, isn't it? Nowadays, advertisers know that a lot of women just want to look as good as possible. Firms often back up their claims with lots of scientific sounding words – and even in this very straightforward ad, they still manage to get in the word **'formula'**.

15

Modern advertising

Advertising went through a huge change in the 1950s and 1960s. This is partly because everyone had radios and they had also started buying televisions.

More and more advertising agencies – which write the adverts for companies – started up. They began to feel that it was important for adverts to be interesting and artistic, otherwise they would just bore people.

- The first advertising-sponsored radio programme, called 'The Eveready Hour' was aired on February 12, 1924, in America
- The first radio programmes to **broadcast** adverts in Britain were heard in 1973 when the LBC channel in London opened
- The first television advert in Britain was for Gibbs SR toothpaste in 1955. It was so boring that one journalist writing in *The Times* newspaper the next day said he'd already forgotten the brand name!

3,000,000 tingling-fresh mouths this morning with

NEW "TINGLING-FRESH" S.R.!

Gibbs SR keeps mouth fresh and gums healthy

Think small.

18 New York University students have gotten into a sun-roof VW; a tight fit. The Volkswagen is sensibly sized for a family. Mother, father, and three growing kids suit it nicely.

In economy runs, the VW averages close to 50 miles per gallon. You won't do near that; after all, professional drivers have canny trade secrets. (Want to know some? Write VW,

Box #65, Englewood, N. J.) Use regular gas and forget about oil between changes.

The VW is 4 feet shorter than a conventional car (yet has as much leg room up front). While other cars are doomed to roam the crowded streets, you park in tiny places.

VW spare parts are inexpensive. A new front fender (at an authorized VW dealer) is

$21.75.* A cylinder head, $19.95.* The nice thing is, they're seldom needed.

A new Volkswagen sedan is $1,565.* Other than a radio and side view mirror, that includes everything you'll really need.

In 1959 about 120,000 Americans thought small and bought VWs. Think about it.

At a time when American cars were getting bigger and bigger a New York agency created adverts for Volkswagen cars which showed a very small car on a huge white page. The slogan was 'Think small.'

People had become fed up with reading other adverts which made fantastic claims about products. They liked the way Volkswagen adverts told the facts about the cars in a simple and believable way. They also thought the Volkswagen advert was funny – and it made them buy the car.

*SUGGESTED RETAIL PRICE, EAST COAST, P.O.E. ©1960 VOLKSWAGEN

Think small.

18 New York University students have gotten into a sun-roof VW; a tight fit. The Volkswagen is sensibly sized for a family. Mother, father, and three growing kids suit it nicely.

In economy runs, the VW averages close to 50 miles per gallon. You won't do near that; after all, professional drivers have canny trade secrets. (Want to know some? Write VW,

Box #65, Englewood, N. J.) Use regular gas and forget about oil between changes.

The VW is 4 feet shorter than a conventional car (yet has as much leg room up front). While other cars are doomed to roam the crowded streets, you park in tiny places.

VW spare parts are inexpensive. A new front fender (at an authorized VW dealer) is

$21.75.* A cylinder head, $19.95.* The nice thing is, they're seldom needed.

A new Volkswagen sedan is $1,565.* Other than a radio and side view mirror, that includes everything you'll really need.

In 1959 about 120,000 Americans thought small and bought VWs. Think about it.

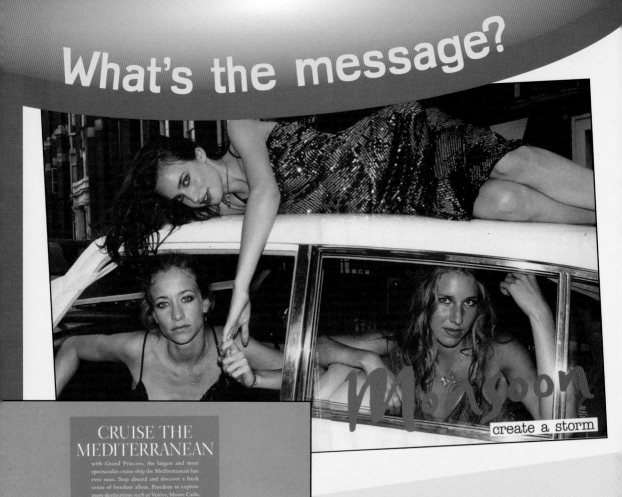

Monsoon

create a storm

CRUISE THE
MEDITERRANEAN

with Grand Princess, the largest and most
spectacular cruise ship the Mediterranean has
ever seen. Step aboard and discover a fresh
sense of freedom afloat. Freedom to explore
more destinations such as Venice, Monte Carlo,
Florence, Barcelona and Istanbul - if you can
be tempted ashore. Freedom to choose when,
where and with whom you dine on board.
And freedom to enjoy your own personal space,
with more rooms offering a private balcony.
While her size may be great, Grand Princess
has the feel of a small, intimate ship with a
personality to match. 12 night cruises start from
just £1,836 per person next summer. In the
Mediterranean, there's only one way to cruise

IN GRAND STYLE.

There is so much advertising
these days that it is easy to take
it all for granted. It is sometimes
hard to remember that firms
spend a lot of money on trying to
get you to spend yours. When you
read adverts, what are they really
telling you? Are you really going
to look cool if you have the same
pair of trainers that someone
famous wears? What happens
if they don't suit you?

18

Pick up any advert and look at the way it is written and photographed. The first thing to think about is who the advert is for. If it is an advert for a toy or sweets or a kind of breakfast cereal it will be made to appeal to children. It could have a cartoon character in it, bright colours and pictures of happy children.

48 new figures to collect !

www.microstars.co.uk

© The Football Association Limited 2003. The FA Crest and FA England Crest are official trade marks of the Football Association Limited and are the subject of extensive trade mark registrations worldwide

Adverts often have persuasive words like 'surely', 'of course', 'it's so easy'. And of course there might be some of those scientific words in there too.

Werther's Original

e Recipe for Success

BBC

Bob the Builder

Buy our new books, videos and magazine OUT NOW!

Can we fix it? Yes, we can!

Slogans

Slogans have always been important in advertising. They are simple ways of getting a person to remember a product. One of the earliest slogans that lots of people remember is:

"YOUR COUNTRY NEEDS YOU"

This poster went up everywhere in Britain at the beginning of **World War One**.

Some slogans are very easy to understand. An advert for beer in the 1930s read 'Guinness is good for you'. It stopped being used when rules came in saying this was a false claim – because alcohol couldn't be good for you. Then the slogan 'Pure Genius' was used. Why do you think this works so well?

Look at these other slogans:

'My Mate'

(Marmite sandwich spread)

'It's the real thing' (Coke)

'Just do it' (Nike sportswear)

Why do we remember these? They are all catchy, but why do they make us want to buy the things they advertise?

How to write your own advert

Are you an advertising company's dream? Try our **Good Buy/ Bad Buy quiz.**

1. How many slogans do you know?
   a) 5 or more
   b) one or two
   c) none.

2. How many times have you got your mum and dad to buy things for you because you've seen them on TV?
   a) all the time
   b) occasionally
   c) never.

3. Do you believe what adverts tell you?
   a) of course
   b) not all the time
   c) never, they'll say anything to make me spend my money.

4. Do you think that adverts show how real people live?
   a) I'd like to live that way
   b) not everybody is like that
   c) of course not, they're all actors.

5. Do you have a favourite advert?
   a) loads
   b) well, one
   c) I never look at adverts.

How did you do? If your answers were mostly a), you're an advertisement company's dream customer; if mostly b), you obviously think for yourself and, if mostly c), who are you kidding?

- Children in Britain watch an average of 20,000 TV adverts every year.
- American children will watch 350,000 adverts by the time they are 18.
- There are no laws about children's advertising in the UK.

Glossary

Index

broadcast – to announce

empire – a time in history when Britain ruled many countries

formula – a list of ingredients to make people think highly of a product

high-tech – advanced electronics

industrial revolution – an era from the late 1800s when machines were used to produce goods on a large scale

persuade – to give reasons for convincing someone to do something

product – an article for sale

snobbery – a belief held by a person that his or her tastes are better than other people's

symbol – a mark that stands for something

World War One – the war known as the Great War which occurred between 1914–18.